*Sugar Inspirations*

# Christmas Figures

## LINDA PAWSEY

MEREHURST

# Dedication

This book is dedicated to my friends and family, particularly Kate and Ian, who have always been there for me with their love and friendship.
Thank you.

Reprinted 1999

Published 1995 by Merehurst Limited
Ferry House, 51–57 Lacy Road, Putney,
London SW15 1PR

A catalogue record for this book is available from the
British Library.

Editor: Helen Southall
Design: Anita Ruddell
Photography by Alan Marsh

Typeset by Servis Filmsetting Ltd, Manchester
Colour separation by P & W Graphics Pty Ltd, Singapore
Printed in Hong Kong by Wing King Tong

# Contents

# Introduction

For centuries we have used our hands to fashion everything from basic clay pots to elaborate sculptures. However simple, a piece of work moulded by hand is always a joy to make and to receive.

The sugar figures and models in this book are made using basic skills with some interesting techniques and finishes. They can be used on Christmas cakes or as table centrepieces, or simply as decorative Christmas ornaments to give as gifts or to keep.

I am never more at peace than when I am making my figures and models. It is an outlet for my creativity that I find most rewarding. With the help of this book I hope you, too, will be able to share my pleasure.

## Equipment

The following equipment is used throughout this book. Specific items required only for certain pieces are detailed where relevant: Non-stick rolling pin and board; Selection of paintbrushes, including a fine one; Cranked pallete knife; Craft knife or scalpel; Ball modelling tool; Thin skewer or modelling pins; Fine scissors; Curved-blade modelling tool; Greaseproof paper (parchment) piping bags; Piping tubes (tips); Cocktail sticks (toothpicks); Straight-tipped tweezers; Different-sized drinking straws; Food colourings and dusting powders (petal dust/blossom tints).

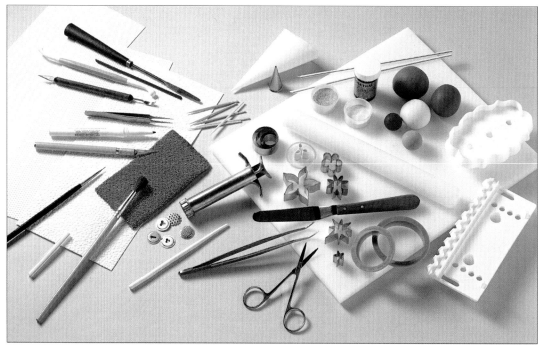

# Modelling Paste

The paste used throughout this book is a half-and-half mixture of sugarpaste (ready-to-roll icing) and flower paste (gum paste). Both can be bought in supermarkets or specialist cake-decorating shops. Whether you use a commercial or homemade flower paste is entirely a matter of personal preference. The pro-portions can be varied slightly depending on whether you pre-fer a firm or soft paste to work with. Remember, however, that a piece made from a greater proportion of sugarpaste will take much longer to dry.

# Modelling Tips

* Whatever modelling medium you choose, it is important that the end result has a smooth, clean surface, free of cracks.

* As most of the moulding and shaping in this book is done by hand, it is essential to keep them very clean. Any dirt or colouring on your hands will be absorbed by the paste as soon as it is worked. For the same reason, keep all equipment and work surfaces clean.

* When shaping pieces by hand, a tiny amount of white vegetable fat on your fingers will help achieve a smooth finish and pre-vent paste sticking.

* For rolled-out pieces, use a non-stick board and rolling pin. If a dusting medium is needed, a small quantity of cornflour or icing (confectioner's) sugar can be used with modelling paste, but remember to use icing sugar only for dusting when working with marzipan (almond paste).

* Whether pieces are assembled after drying or while still soft is very much personal choice. If arms, for example, are dried before being attached to the body, it is vital that they are moulded into the required fin-ished position before being set aside to dry.

* A wide variety of tools and tex-ture pads is now available. These can be used to great effect. Animal fur and wool and textile finishes are easy to achieve.

# Colouring

Modelling paste can be coloured in three different ways:

**1** Knead paste or liquid food colouring into the model-ling paste until it is the required colour.

**2** Combine white flower paste (bought or home-made) with ready-coloured sugarpaste.

**3** Paint on colour after drying. This is particularly useful for facial features, such as eyebrows and lips, and also for highlighting or emphasizing details (pockets, creases, hair, etc.). Use diluted paste food colouring and a fine paintbrush.

# Drying and Assembly

The amount of time pieces need to be left to dry depends on many things – temperature, humidity, type of paste used – but as a general guide allow at least 24 hours, bearing in mind that some pieces might require longer. Lie pieces to dry on a piece of sponge or foam so the air can circulate around them, supporting if necessary with pieces of foam or tissue.

When assembling body parts, etc., secure them in posi-tion with sugarpaste glue or tiny amounts of modelling paste soft-ened with sugarpaste glue or egg white. To make sugarpaste glue, break 60g (2oz) sugarpaste into small pieces and put it in a heatproof bowl with 2½ table-spoons water. Heat in a micro-wave or over a saucepan of hot water, stirring occasionally, until the sugarpaste has dissolved. Store in a clean con-tainer. To use, apply sparingly with a paintbrush. Other edible glues can be used but sugarpaste glue is useful because it does not dry with a shine.

### Tip

Flesh-coloured paste is used for many of the figures in this book. A good flesh colour can be achieved by kneading tiny amounts of chestnut brown colouring into the paste.

# Shaping Figures

Most modelling begins with one of three basic shapes – a cone, ball or sausage. In addition to these, a T-shape can be used which incorporates body and arms in one piece. With practice, this can be extended to include legs, feet and hands as well, giving a much stronger, all-in-one piece.

## Sizes

When deciding what size of finished model to make, an important consideration is whether or not your model is to be free-standing or to be used as a cake ornament. If several figures are to be used on a cake, they should be small enough not to overwhelm the cake on which they will stand. As an approximate guide, a 60g (2oz) piece of paste will make a body of about 7.5cm (3 inches) in length (excluding the head). A 30g (1oz) ball of paste will make a 5cm (2 inch) body.

## Simple Figure

A simple body shape can be made without sleeves (arms) from a basic cone shape.

**1** Roll the required amount of modelling paste (see page 5) into a smooth, crack-free ball. Roll the ball between the palms of your hands to make a cone shape.

**2** Flatten the base of the cone so that the figure will stand freely. With thumb and index finger slightly moist-ened with white vegetable fat, gently stroke around the base and sides of the piece to form a thin edge (the hem of the garment).

**3** While the body shape is still soft, use a skewer to make a hole in the top for the neck, and also on either side to hold the sleeves.

### Sleeves

**4** Using pea-sized pieces of paste, roll two cone shapes half the length of the body. At the thicker end of each, pinch out a small peg. Using a skewer, open up the narrow end of the cone for the sleeve opening.

**5** Brush some sugarpaste glue (see page 5) inside the armholes in the body and attach the sleeves. Frilling or indenting the ends of the sleeves gives a variety of styles.

## T-Shape Figure

This figure incorporates the body and sleeves (arms) in one piece.

**1** Roll the ball of paste into a sausage shape that is slightly thicker at one end. Pinch out the paste on either side of the thicker end to form the arms, and roll gently between finger and thumb to lengthen.

**2** Level the base and smooth the edges to form a fine hem as for the Simple Figure (step 2). Open the ends of the sleeves and make a neck hole in the top as for the Simple Figure.

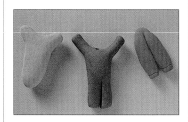

### Trousers

Trousers can be incorporated in the T-Shape Figure by cutting up the centre of the base. Use a skewer to open both ends to accommodate shoes.

For separate trousers, use half the amount of paste used for the figure and roll into a sausage about 10cm (4 inches) long. Thin out the centre of the sausage by rolling with one finger. Open both ends to form the ends of the trousers and, while still soft, fold the piece in half, bringing the ends together.

### Jumpers and jackets

To make these separately, make shorter versions of either the Simple Figure or the T-Shape Figure and open out at the base.

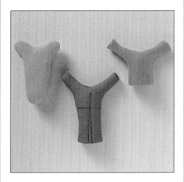

## All-in-one Body Shape

This method incorporates body and legs in one piece. It is suitable for figures whose clothing needs to be added separately because it is more detailed and a little finer. The arms (with hands) are made separately and attached with softened modelling paste (see page 5) after the figure has been dressed.

### Body and legs

 For a figure about 13cm (5 inches) high, mould a 30g (1oz) piece of flesh-coloured modelling paste into a thick sausage shape. Roll and thin

each end until it is about half the thickness of the middle.

**2** For the ankles, roll again to thin a short way in from each end of the paste. Gently pinch the ends and at the same time bend to form feet.

**3** While still soft, bend the paste in the middle and

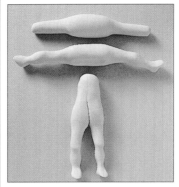

bring the legs down. Squeeze the paste on the top of each leg to form knees. Roll the paste in the centre to thin it slightly and form a waist. Coax the legs into whatever position is required, standing or sitting.

**4** Use a skewer to make holes in the top and sides of the body for the head and arms. Set aside to dry.

### Arms

**5** Roll a small piece of flesh-coloured paste into a tapered sausage, the wider end forming the shoulder and upper arm. Thin the paste at the narrow end to form a wrist and flatten the tip to create an oval shape for the hand. Cut the fingers and thumb with fine scissors.

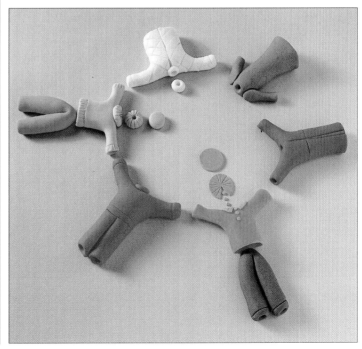

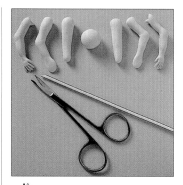

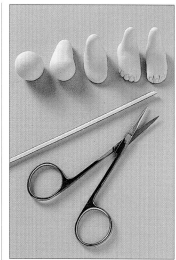

enough to fit into the arm hole on the body. Repeat to make a second arm, then leave both to dry.

## Toes

**7** Toe nails can be marked with a thin drinking straw cut to the shape of a nail. Mark the end of the foot and cut with a craft knife or scalpel to separate the toes.

## Head

**8** Detailed instructions for making a head can be found on page 20.

**6** Gently bend the arm and pinch lightly to make the elbow. On the inside of the shoulder, pinch out a piece of paste to form a post small

# Santa's Aching Feet

*After a busy Christmas Eve,*
*a hard-working Santa takes a well-earned rest.*

## Materials

185g (6oz) white modelling
paste (see page 5)
Red, black and chestnut brown
paste food colourings
Raw dried spaghetti
Sugarpaste glue (see page 5)
Softened modelling paste (see
page 5)
Piping jelly

## Equipment

Curved-blade modelling tool

### Trousers and jacket

**1** Colour 125g (4oz)
modelling paste red and
divide it in half. Mould one half
into a pair of trousers following
the instructions on page 7. Bend
the piece at the knees so the fin-
ished figure can be seated. Mark
'creases' round the legs so that
it looks like the trousers are
rolled up. Set aside to dry.

**2** Save a small piece of the
remaining red paste for
the hat and shape the rest to
make a long jacket with separate sleeves (see page 7). Curve
the sleeves so they can be posi-
tioned with the hands clasped
behind Santa's head. Ensure
that the jacket fits snugly over

the top of the trousers, then set
aside the separate pieces to dry
thoroughly.

### Head and hands

**3** Colour 15g (½ oz)
modelling paste flesh-
coloured (see page 5) and make
a pair of hands and a head (see
pages 20 and 21). Mark an open
mouth and closed eyes on to the
face, and ease a piece of dried
spaghetti up inside the neck for
extra support. Set aside to dry.

**4** Roll out some white
modelling paste and cut a
piece for Santa's hair (see page
21). Attach to the head and
leave to dry.

**5** For the beard, mould a
Y-shaped piece of white
paste and mark it all over with
the curved-blade tool. Shape it
to fit the face and set aside to
dry. (The beard should not be
attached to Santa's face until
after the figure has been assembled.)

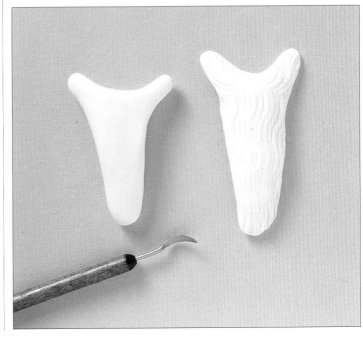

**9**

### Hat and feet

**6** Using the reserved piece of red paste, make a hat trimmed with white paste as shown on page 38. Using sugarpaste glue, attach the hat to the dried head. (The edge of the jacket can be trimmed with white in the same way as the hat.)

**7** Mould two feet (see page 8) from flesh-coloured paste ensuring that the ankles will fit inside the trousers.

### Finishing

**8** Using softened modelling paste, assemble the dried pieces of Santa.

**9** For Santa's chair, cut a small square cake using a template made from the outline on page 47.

**10** The bowl is made by hollowing out a ball of paste and turning back the edges. Piping jelly is used for

the water. For Santa's boots, see page 39; for Christmas presents, see page 34.

# Sledging Fun

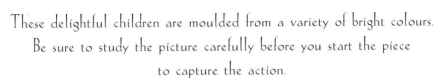

These delightful children are moulded from a variety of bright colours.
Be sure to study the picture carefully before you start the piece
to capture the action.

## Materials

470g (15oz) modelling paste
(see page 5)
Blue, pink, green, orange, yellow
and brown paste food colourings
Sugarpaste glue (see page 5)
Softened modelling paste (see
page 5)
60g (2oz) brown flower paste

## Equipment

Straight-tipped tweezers
No. 3 piping tube (tip)
2.5cm (1 inch) round briar rose
cutter
Plaque cutter or template

## Preparation

**1** Divide the modelling paste into portions and colour as follows: three 30g (1oz) pieces blue, mauve and pink; four 60g (2oz) pieces green, yellow, light brown and flesh-colour; 90g (3oz) orange.

**2** Set aside small quantities from each of the colours for collars, buttons, scarves, etc.

## Trousers

**3** Using 30g (1oz) pieces of paste, and following the instructions on page 7, make five pairs of trousers in the following colours: one each in light brown, orange and blue, and two in green. Gently bend three of the pieces at the knees to enable the finished figures to be seated. Set aside to dry.

## Jumpers and jackets

**4** Mould two tops from 30g (1oz) pieces of mauve and orange paste, following the instructions on page 6 for a T-Shape figure. Roll out and cut 2.5cm (1 inch) circles from each of the colours for collars. With straight-tipped tweezers, pinch around the edges and attach over the neck holes. Score around the bottoms of the jumpers and the sleeve ends to make welts.

**5** To make a quilted jacket, form a T-shaped top as before from 30g (1oz) pink paste. Score the centre front to form an opening and mark diagonal lines across the sleeves and body section to give a quilted effect.

**6** Roll out a small piece of paste and cut out eight small buttons using a no. 3 piping tube. Attach to the jacket. Flatten a small ball shape to form a rolled collar. Attach to the top of the jacket and make a hole for the neck with a skewer.

**7** Repeat steps 5 and 6 to make a second quilted jacket, using light brown paste. Make a third, plain, jacket from orange paste. Attach the jumpers and jackets to the pairs of trousers, carefully moulding the soft paste on to the dried trousers to give a smooth finish. Set aside to dry.

### Ski suit

**8** Using the yellow paste, make an all-in-one figure as shown on page 7.

### Heads and hands

**9** Following the detailed instructions on pages 20 and 21, mould six heads and three pairs of hands from flesh-coloured modelling paste. Allow to dry thoroughly for at least 24 hours.

**10** Make three pairs of mittens and matching hats and scarves following the instructions on pages 38 and 39, using the reserved pieces of coloured modelling paste.

### Shoes and sledge

**11** The shoes are moulded from brown flower paste (see page 39).

**12** The sledge is cut from brown flower paste using either a plaque cutter or a template made from the outline on page 46.

### Finishing

**13** Attach the heads, hands, shoes, etc., with softened modelling paste.

**14** To make the snowy slopes, make a template from the outline on page 47 and use it to cut a 30cm (12 inch) round cake to the right shape. Cover with marzipan (almond paste) and sugarpaste.

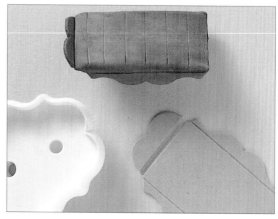

# Postie's Dilemma

This fun figure is ideal for a family table centrepiece
or for when only a small cake is required.

## Materials

280g (9oz) modelling paste (see
page 5)
Blue, brown and red paste food
colourings
Raw dried spaghetti
Sugarpaste glue (see page 5)
Softened modelling paste (see
page 5)
6 small sweets

## Equipment

2.5cm (1 inch) and 4cm (1½
inch) round cutters
Black, blue and red food colouring pens
No. 3 piping tube (tip)

### Trousers and jacket

**1** Colour 155g (5oz)
modelling paste blue.
Following the instructions on
page 7, mould 60g (2oz) of the
blue paste into a pair of
trousers. Bend the legs slightly
to give movement. Push a piece
of spaghetti into each leg for
strength and mark 'turn-ups' at
the end of each leg. Set aside to
dry for 48 hours.

**2** Using the method on page
7, mould a jacket and separate sleeves from another 60g
(2oz) blue paste. Bend the
sleeves and mark creases at the
elbows. Allow to dry thoroughly.

**3** Colour about 15g (½ oz)
paste red. Roll out a small
piece and cut out a 2.5cm (1
inch) round collar and two thin
strips. Roll and cut another
2.5cm (1 inch) circle from blue
paste, trim a little off around the
edge and place on top of the red
collar. Cut two blue pockets.
Attach red stripes along the tops
of the pockets and around the
ends of the sleeves. Buttons may
also be added.

### Head, hands and hat

**4** Colour 30g (1oz)
modelling paste flesh-
coloured (see page 7). Mould a
head and hands (see pages 20
and 21), giving the face a

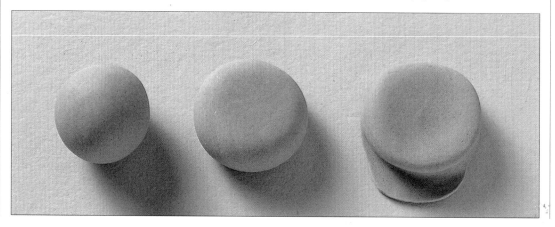

shocked look. Allow to dry for at least 24 hours.

⟨5⟩ From a piece of blue paste, mould a flattened ball shape. Roll one side to form a peak. Attach to the dried head with sugarpaste glue.

### Assembly

⟨6⟩ Join all the pieces together with softened modelling paste. See the picture on page 15 for guidance when positioning the arms and hands.

### Letters and parcels

⟨7⟩ Roll out a piece of white modelling paste and cut out 30 rectangles measuring 1cm (½ inch) wide by 1.5cm (¾ inch) long. Mark a V shape on one side of half of the envelopes and on the other half mark small addresses and stamps using food colouring pens. When dried, attach a letter to one of the hands.

⟨8⟩ Colour 30g (1oz) modelling paste dark brown and roll out. Cut out an oblong for the sack using a template made from the outline on page 46. Fold as shown, placing small sweets inside. Cut and attach a strap.

⟨9⟩ Make the parcels from light brown paste (see page 34).

### Finishing

⟨10⟩ The post box can be made either from a Swiss roll (jelly roll) or from two 7.5cm (3 inch) circles of fruit cake, stacked one on top of the other. Cover with marzipan (almond paste) and red sugarpaste.

# Choral Cuties

These adorable little choirboys in their bright red cassocks
will brighten any festive table.

## Materials

345g (11oz) white modelling
paste (see page 5)
Red, brown, cream and green
paste food colourings
Sugarpaste glue (see page 5)
Softened modelling paste (see
page 5)
Christmas tree and presents
(see page 34)

## Equipment

5cm (2 inch) and 2.5cm (1 inch)
round cutters
Frilling tool or cocktail stick
(toothpick)
Black food colouring pen
Greaseproof paper (parchment)
piping bag

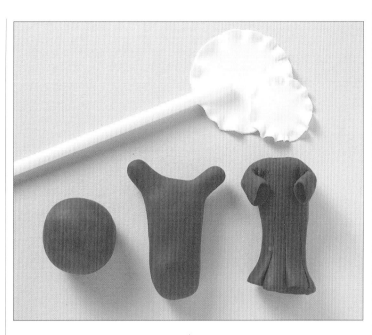

### Cassocks

**1** Colour 185g (6oz)
modelling paste red. Using
a 30g (1oz) ball of red paste,
mould a T-shaped body with
sleeves (see page 6). Mark folds
in the cassock.

**2** Repeat to make five more
choirboys, using 30g (1oz)
paste for each one. Support the
arms in different positions with
pieces of foam or tissue paper,
and set aside to dry for 48
hours.

### Surplices

**3** Roll out a thin piece of
white modelling paste and
cut out one 5cm (2 inch) circle
and one 2.5cm (1 inch) circle.
Frill the edges of both pieces by
rolling with a frilling tool or
cocktail stick.

**4** Using sugarpaste glue,
attach and drape the larg-
er frill over the shoulders of one
figure and attach the smaller
frill on top. Make a neck hole in
the frilled collar.

> **5** Repeat steps 3 and 4 for the other choirboys and leave them all to dry.

## Heads

> **6** Colour 60g (2oz) modelling paste flesh-coloured (see page 7) and make six heads (see page 20). Allow to dry. Paint on facial details and add hair as shown, using cream and brown modelling paste. Attach carefully to the bodies with softened modelling paste.

## Hymn books

> **7** Colour about 15g (½ oz) modelling paste green and roll it out quite thinly. Using white paste, roll out a slightly thicker piece and glue this on top of the green.

> **8** Cut several rectangles measuring 2.5 x 1cm (1 x ½ inch), and fold in half to form hymn books. While still soft, open some books out fully. Set aside to dry.

> **9** Using a black food colouring pen, write 'Hymn Book' on the covers and lines of music on the inside pages.

## Hands

> **10** Using the remaining flesh-coloured paste, make six pairs of hands (see page 21). It is important to make these last so they can be moulded around the hymn books while still soft. Set aside to dry.

> **11** Put some softened modelling paste into a greaseproof paper piping bag, snip off the tip and pipe the paste into the ends of the sleeves. Attach the hands and hymn books. Place the dried choirboys flat and support the hands with foam until they, too, have dried thoroughly in position.

## Finishing

> **12** The choirboys can be used on any shape of cake; a two-tier cake is very effective. A Christmas tree and gifts (see page 34) can be added for extra colour.

# Heads and Hands

To give life to your figures it is important that faces are attractive and full of character. Even with simple figures, you can vary the head shape, nose size, etc., to achieve a wide variety of expressive faces.

## Materials

Flesh-coloured modelling paste (see page 5)
Raw dried spaghetti (optional)
Sugarpaste glue (see page 5)
Brown, cream or white modelling paste
Red and brown paste food colourings
Plum dusting powder (petal dust/blossom tint)
Cornflour

## Equipment

Drinking straws
Round-ended modelling pin
Cocktail sticks (toothpicks)
Curved-blade modelling tool
Daisy cutters
Round briar rose cutters
Fine scissors
Paintbrushes, including a fine sable

### Heads

**1** Making heads free-hand might take a little practice but the end result will be worthwhile. Mould a piece of flesh-coloured paste into a smooth ball shape. Place the ball in the palm of one hand and, with the index finger of the other hand, roll lightly across the centre until a fat peanut shape is achieved.

**2** Pinch the paste at the lower back of the head to form a neck. A piece of raw dried spaghetti can be inserted into the neck to give extra strength.

**3** By changing the position of the finger when rolling the paste it is possible to shape fat chins and narrow foreheads and vice versa. (For babies and small children, a ball shape alone may suffice.)

**4** A very easy way to mark the eyes, eyebrows and mouth is to use the end of a drinking straw.

### Ears

**5** Attach a small cone of paste to either side of the head while still soft. Press the narrow end of each cone gently into the head with a small round-ended modelling pin or the end of a paintbrush to hollow out the inner ear.

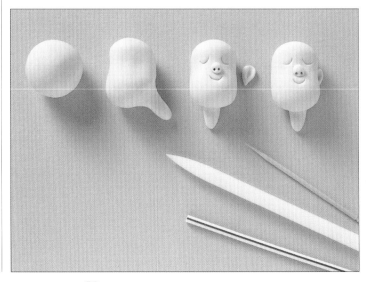

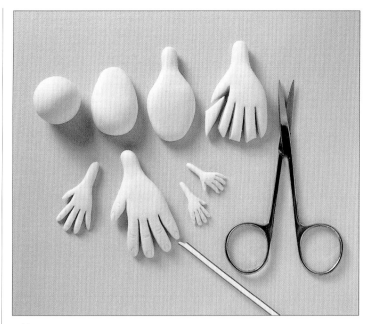

## Painting

⟨9⟩ Allow heads to dry completely before painting. Use well diluted paste colours and a very fine paintbrush. To give a blush to the cheeks, use plum dusting powder mixed with cornflour.

## Hands

⟨10⟩ From a smooth ball of flesh-coloured paste form a flattened cone with a narrow end for the wrist. Using fine scissors, cut a small V shape from one side for the thumb, and make three further cuts for the fingers. On larger hands, mark fingernails with the end of a straw.

⟨6⟩ Another way to make ears is to insert the modelling pin into the side of the head and to ease a small amount of paste out to the side.

## Noses

⟨7⟩ Ball shapes or cones form dainty or comical noses. Mark nostrils with a cocktail stick after attaching the nose to the face with a tiny amount of sugarpaste glue.

## Hair

⟨8⟩ Various hairstyles can be accomplished by texturing and scoring the rolled-out paste in different ways. A curved-blade modelling tool is very useful. Daisy cutters and small round briar rose cutters are ideal shapes for cutting the rolled-out paste for hair.

# Teddies Galore

*A sack of Christmas teddy bears makes a charming addition to any festive table.*

## Materials

185g (6oz) white modelling paste (see page 5)
Cream, red and black paste food colourings
Raw dried spaghetti
Sugarpaste glue (see page 5)
White vegetable fat
Confectioner's glaze
Brown sugarpaste (ready-to-roll icing)
Softened modelling paste (see page 5)

## Equipment

Texture pad or flat plastic scourer
Curved-blade modelling tool
Ball modelling tool

### Heads

**1** Colour 155g (5oz) modelling paste dark cream. Form a 30g (1oz) piece of cream paste into a ball shape. Roll lightly on a texture pad or flat plastic scourer to give a curly fur effect.

**2** With finger and thumb, ease some paste on one side of the ball into a rounded peak to form a snout. Cut an inverted curved T shape for the mouth using the blade tool.

Pinch a small amount of paste under the head to form a neck and insert a short piece of raw, dried spaghetti to give added strength, if liked.

### Eyes, nose and ears

**3** Use the ball tool to make sockets for the eyes and a small hole for the nose. Roll two tiny balls of cream paste for the eyes and one slightly larger for the nose. Fix them all in position with tiny amounts of sugarpaste glue.

**4** Roll two small balls of cream paste on the texture pad or scourer and then press on one side with the ball

tool. Make an indent on either side of the head and carefully glue on the ears, pressing gently with the ball tool so they stay in position.

**5** Repeat steps 1–4 to make one more head from a 30g (1oz) piece of paste, then two more slightly smaller heads. Set aside to dry for at least 24 hours.

### Hands

**6** Make four pairs of hands (see page 21), pressing each gently on the texture pad or scourer. Curl the fingers over slightly, and allow to dry in that position.

### Painting

**7** Mix some white vegetable fat with a small quantity of cream paste food colouring and paint the dried heads and hands. With absorbent kitchen paper, wipe off the surplus colour and set aside to dry. Paint the nose, eyes and mouth with black paste food colouring. When dry, glaze the eyes and nose with confectioner's glaze.

### Hats

**8** Following the instructions on page 38, and using 15g (½oz) each of red and white paste, make two Santa Claus hats and two party hats. Fix to the teddies' heads.

### Finishing

**9** For the teddies' sack, trim the sides of a 10cm (4 inch) round cake using a template made from the outline on page 47. Roll out and cut an oblong of brown textured sugarpaste and lay it over the cake, joining the paste at the sides. Position the teddies' heads and hands and secure with softened modelling paste. Added decorations, such as holly (see page 41) and ribbons (see page 34), give extra appeal. Place the cake on a board covered with sugarpaste.

# Nativity

A two-tier cake provides just the right setting for this traditional scene.

## Materials

550g (18oz) white modelling paste (see page 5)
Purple, red, yellow, gold, cream, dark brown and blue paste food colourings
Lustre dusting powders
30g (1oz) cream flower paste
Sugarpaste glue (see page 5)
1 tablespoon royal icing
Softened modelling paste (see page 5)

## Equipment

1cm (½ inch) briar rose cutter
Lace cutter
Cocktail stick (toothpick)
Star cutter
Large calyx cutter
Small greaseproof paper (parchment) piping bag
28-gauge wire
Brown florist's tape

### The Three Kings

**1** Colour 30g (1oz) modelling paste purple, 30g (1oz) red and 30g (1oz) yellow. From each of the three pieces, cut off a quarter and reserve for sleeves and collars. Following the instructions on page 6, mould separate bodies and sleeves from each of the three colours.

**2** The collars and capes are made from rolled and frilled circles (cut with the briar rose cutter) and squares topped with small flattened ball shapes for the necks. The crowns are cut from white paste with a lace cutter (see page 38).

**3** From small pieces of white paste, mould tiny gifts. Score around the top for lids and ease out some paste on either side with a cocktail stick for handles. When dry, dust with lustre colour.

### Angels

**4** Form 15g (½oz) white modelling paste into a smooth T-shaped figure (see page 6). Pierce the top to make a neck hole and open up the ends of the sleeves. Allow the figure to dry flat with the arms raised.

**5** Make two more angels, this time easing the arms forward and together. Set aside to dry.

### Trumpet and stars

**6** Roll a small, thin sausage of cream flower paste and open up one end to form a trumpet shape. Paint carefully with gold colouring, and allow to dry.

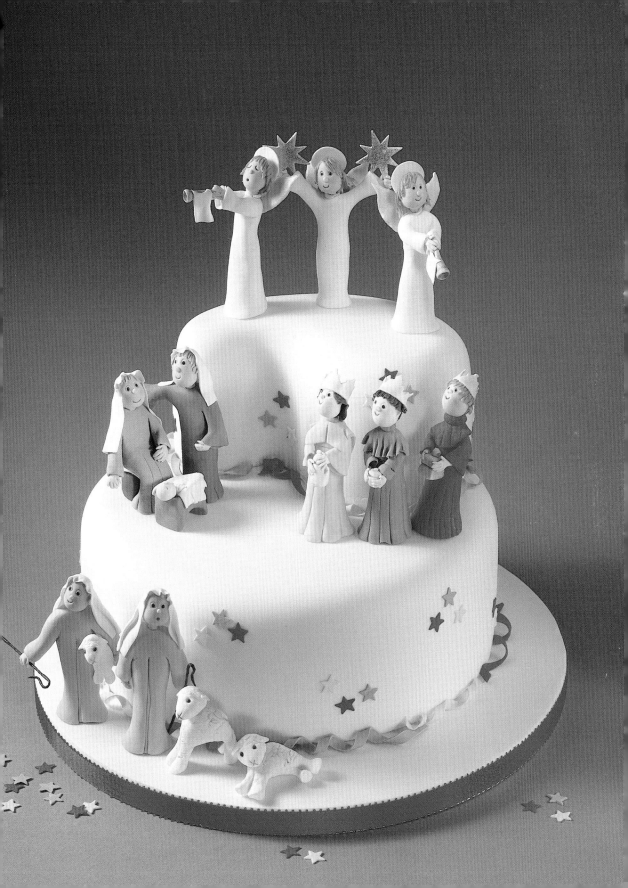

**7** Roll out another piece of flower paste until it is quite thin, and cut a small rectangle for a banner. Attach with sugarpaste glue.

**8** Roll out another piece of cream flower paste and cut out two stars. Paint with gold colouring and leave to dry.

### Wings

**9** Roll out a piece of cream flower paste and cut out two sets of wings, using sections of the calyx cutter. Fold slightly and leave to dry over a piece of sponge.

**10** Dust the wings with gold lustre powder and attach to the backs of the angels using royal icing in a piping bag.

### Shepherds

**11** Colour 90g (3oz) modelling paste light brown. Using the T-shape method shown on page 6 and 30g (1oz) light brown paste,

mould a smooth body shape. Score down the centre front. Make a second shepherd.

**12** For the shepherds' crooks, cover pieces of 28-gauge wire with brown florist's tape and bend the tops.

### Mary and Joseph

**13** Using 30g (1oz) blue paste, and following the instructions on page 6, mould a T-shaped body for Mary and, while still soft, gently bend the figure in the middle so that it can be seated.

**14** Make another T-shaped figure from 30g (1oz) dark brown paste for Joseph and raise one arm so that it will rest on Mary's shoulder. Shape a small light brown box shape for Mary to sit on.

### Heads and hands

**15** Colour 90g (3oz) modelling paste flesh-coloured (see page 5) and make

heads and hands for all the figures (see pages 20 and 21). Attach the angels' and Three Kings' hands while still soft so they can be moulded around the trumpet, stars and gifts. Leave the rest to dry.

**16** For the head-dresses, cut small oblongs of rolled-out white paste, and mould them around the heads of the shepherds, Mary and Joseph. Cut out two tiny white halos using the 1cm (½ inch) rose cutter. Add one to each angel's head.

### Lambs

**17** The lambs are moulded from small pieces of white paste. The heads are moulded separately and attached when the bodies have dried.

### Baby Jesus

**18** From a tiny piece of flesh-coloured paste, make a head, body and hands. For the crib, mould a small oblong from a piece of light brown paste and pinch out legs. Hollow out the top. Roll out and cut a small blanket from cream paste.

### Finishing

**19** Using softened modelling paste, assemble all the figures and set aside to dry.

**20** A two-tier cake allows all the figures to be displayed without overcrowding. Finish the decoration with streamers (see page 35). Remember that items painted gold must not be eaten.

# Christmas Mouse

This sweet little character would be welcome at any
Christmas party. A good picture or model for reference is always helpful
when shaping animals.

## Materials

90g (3oz) white modelling paste
(see page 5)
Cream, red and black paste food
colourings
Sugarpaste glue (see page 5)
Softened modelling paste (see
page 5)
Confectioner's glaze
White vegetable fat

## Equipment

Curved-blade modelling tool

### Body and head

**1** Colour 60g (2oz)
modelling paste pale
cream and roll it into a thick
sausage 7.5cm (3 inches) long.
Roll the paste to thin it slightly
about a quarter of the way down
to form a neck. Gently ease
some paste forward to form a
long thin nose. Mark an inverted, curved T shape for the
mouth and make holes for the
eye sockets.

**2** For ears, colour 15g
(½ oz) modelling paste
flesh-coloured (see page 5).
Flatten and thin two small balls
and attach to the side of the
head with sugarpaste glue,
bending them into cupped ear
shapes.

27

**3** Score all over the body and head with the curved-blade modelling tool to give the impression of fur. Set aside to dry thoroughly.

### Arms

**4** Using a small piece of flesh-coloured paste, roll a thin sausage and taper it at one end. This should be about half the length of the body. Roll a thin wrist and bend and pinch it slightly in the middle to form an elbow.

**5** Following the instructions on page 21, flatten the narrow end of the paste and cut a hand shape with a very small thumb. Repeat to make the other arm. Score both arms to mark the lines of fur.

**6** Make a small gift (see page 34) and use softened modelling paste to attach it to the hands, then attach the arms to the body.

**7** Lie the mouse down and support the arms so that they dry in position. Glue in two black ball shapes for the eyes and brush with glaze.

### Feet and tail

**8** Roll two small pieces of flesh-coloured paste and flatten one half of each. Cut long thin toes. Attach to the under-side of the front of the body while still soft.

**9** Roll a long thin sausage of paste for the tail and score all along it. Flatten one end and attach to the body.

### Finishing

**10** When completely set, brush the body, head and arms with a mixture of white fat and cream food colouring. Leave the front of the body pale.

**11** Mould the hat following the instructions on page 38, and roll a thin strip of black paste for the bow tie.

**12** Cover a cake board with textured white sug-arpaste. Cut a sheet of thin red sugarpaste and arrange it in loose folds in the centre of the board. Stand the mouse in the centre and finish the decoration with holly and ribbons (see pages 41 and 34).

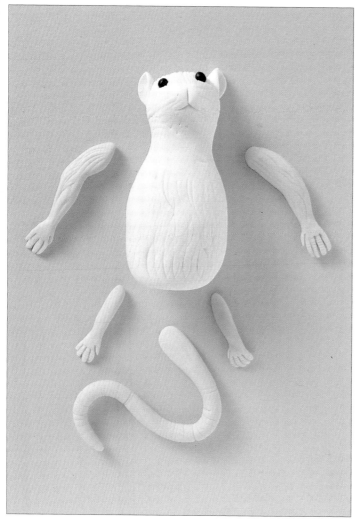

# Sweet Dreams

*A delightful cake to give grandchildren.*
*A sponge cake can be used for the base instead of a fruit cake.*

## Materials

60g (2oz) white modelling paste
(see page 5)
Red, blue, green and brown
paste food colourings
60g (2oz) white sugarpaste
(ready-to-roll icing)

## Equipment

2.5cm (1 inch) daisy cutter
Paintbrush or thin skewer
Clay gun or tea strainer

## Heads and hands

**1** Colour 30g (1oz) modelling paste flesh-coloured (see page 5) and mould three heads (see page 20), one of which should be smaller than the others. When dry, mark and paint the facial details, the smaller head with eyes open and the larger two with eyes closed.

**2** From brown paste, roll and cut daisy shapes for hair (see page 21), and attach to the heads.

**3** Make three sets of hands (see page 21), each with the fingers curling over. Set aside to dry over a large drinking straw.

## Bodies

**4** Mould three cone shapes from white sugarpaste, making each one about two and a half times the length of its head. With the end of a paintbrush or thin skewer, press a T shape into the thicker end of the cone. Pinch together to form feet.

## Hot water bottles and slippers

**5** Mould a small sausage shape from red modelling paste. Flatten into a rounded rectangle and mark the surface to give a quilted effect. Attach a small hollowed-out cone to one end of the bottle and a tiny flattened ball of paste with a hole through it to the other end.

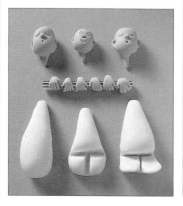

**6** Make two tiny cone shapes, flatten the thicker ends slightly and open out to form slippers. Make two more pairs with different-coloured pastes. Attach bows, or push a small quantity of paste through a clay gun or tea strainer to make small pompoms.

## Finishing

**7** Use an oblong cake for the bed. Cover with marzipan, then a pleated valance made from cream sugarpaste. Place the figures on the bed and cover with a textured and frilled sugarpaste bedspread. Add frilly pillowcases and three modelled Christmas stockings.

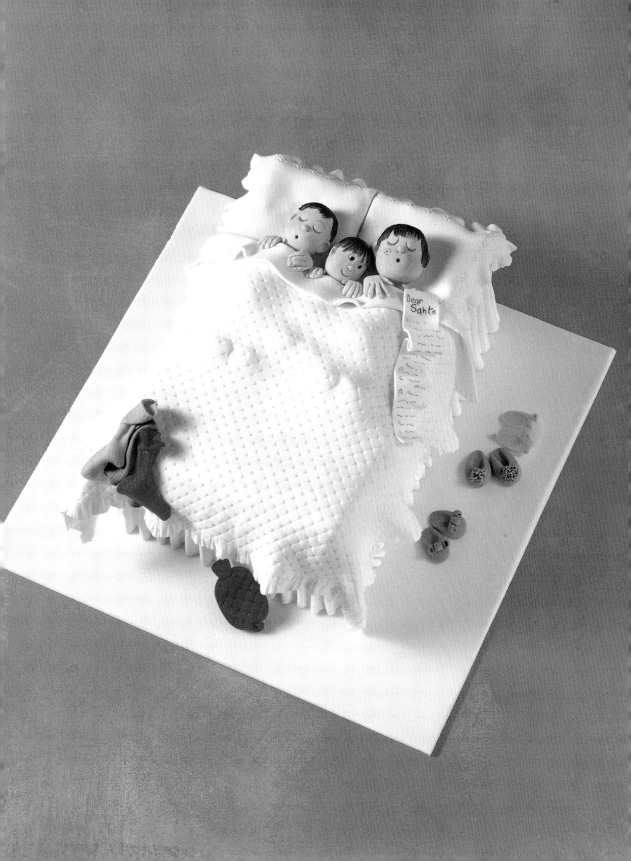

# Chef's Challenge

A fun piece designed to amuse all ages.

## Materials

375g (12oz) white modelling paste (see page 5)
Brown and blue paste food colourings
Softened modelling paste (see page 5)
Miniature Christmas puddings and cakes (see page 40)

## Equipment

No. 3 piping tube (tip)
Squared texture sheet

### Chef's jacket and trousers

**1** Using a 60g (2oz) piece of white modelling paste, make a jacket with separate sleeves and a rolled collar (see page 7). Cut buttons from rolled-out white paste using the piping tube. Allow to dry.

**2** Mould a pair of trousers (see page 7) from another 60g (2oz) piece of white paste and, while still soft, press the front and back on to a squared texture sheet. Bend the trousers so that the figure is sitting down.

**3** When dry, brush the trousers lightly with diluted blue colouring so that checks appear. Leave to dry.

### Head and hands

**4** Colour 15g (½oz) modelling paste flesh-coloured (see page 5) and make a head and hands (see pages 20 and 21).

**5** Divide 125g (4oz) modelling paste in two and colour in two tones of brown. Knead the two lightly together to give two-tone brown paste. Roll out and use to make the chef's hair (see page 21). (The remaining two-tone paste is used for the Christmas puddings.)

### Hat

**6** Mould a piece of white paste into a thick sausage shape. Hollow out one end enough to fit around the chef's head and pinch out the other end to form a folded top. Attach to the head while still soft.

### Finishing

**7** Using softened modelling paste, assemble the dried pieces. Attach the chef to the top of your cake. Almost any size and shape of cake is suitable. Surround him with puddings and cakes (see page 40).

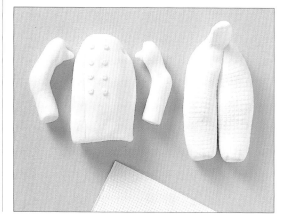

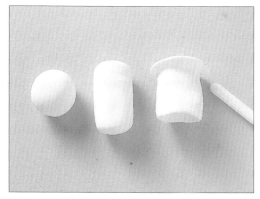

# Christmas Decorations

Additional small items can be added to your cakes
to make them more festive. Here are a few ideas.

## Christmas Presents

Cut a variety of shapes from different coloured batches of modelling paste and score the sides in a V shape to represent the folded ends of wrapping paper. The parcels can be sponged to give a mottled effect. If brushed with lustre powder colour the shapes can be made to look like presents wrapped in metallic paper. Add ribbons and bows (see below).

## Ribbons and Bows

Ribbons are made by cutting very thin strips of coloured flower paste. Bows can be made either by pinching a tiny sausage of paste in the middle with tweezers, or by pushing paste through the fine mesh on a clay gun or through a tea strainer.

## Christmas Trees

Neat work is important when making a Christmas tree so allow enough time to achieve a good result. A variety of sizes can be made. Form a long pointed cone of green paste.

Commencing at the point, cut small, neat V shapes in the paste with fine scissors or by pinching the paste with very fine straight tweezers held at an angle of 45° to the side of the cone. Continue in a circle all around the top, then work down the length of the paste making neat rows of V shapes. Set aside

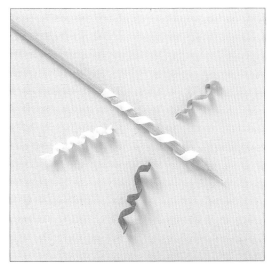

for at least 24 hours until thoroughly dry. The trees can be decorated with piped garlands and small baubles.

# Streamers

Roll out some coloured flower paste and cut thin strips about 7.5cm (3 inches) long. Wrap several strips around drinking straws or fine bamboo skewers in a corkscrew formation. Leave to harden a little for about 2 hours, then carefully slide off and leave to dry completely.

# Happy Families

These very simple snowpeople are fun to make and always popular.
They make a delightful Christmas ornament.

## Materials

280g (9oz) white modelling paste (see page 5)
Softened modelling paste (see page 5)
Raw dried spaghetti
Green, brown, red and yellow paste food colourings
Sugarpaste glue (see page 5)

## Equipment

Drinking straw
Frilling tool or cocktail stick (toothpick)

### Mum and Dad

**1** Mould a 60g (2oz) piece of white modelling paste into a smooth T-shaped figure (see page 6). Make small holes down the front of the body to hold buttons. Repeat to make a second figure, this time raising one arm so that it can rest on the shoulder of the other.

**2** Using small balls of paste, make mitten-shaped hands. When dry, attach to the figures with softened modelling paste.

### Heads

**3** Mould two heads from white paste (see page 20) and mark eyes and mouths with a large drinking straw. Attach small balls of paste for the noses and pinch the bases of the heads to form necks. Insert pieces of spaghetti for strength. When dry, paint in the eyes and mouth.

### Children

**4** Repeat steps 1–3 for the snowchildren, using only 15g (½oz) white paste. Indent the centre front to form legs, and bend to make feet. The little snowgirl's skirt is a strip of thin white paste frilled along one edge with a frilling tool, or cocktail stick, and attached around the waist.

### Finishing

**5** Attach the dried heads with softened modelling paste. Roll and flatten tiny balls of brown paste for the buttons on the front of the bodies. Attach with sugarpaste glue.

**6** Using small pieces of coloured paste, make hats, scarves and earmuffs as shown on pages 38 and 39. Attach to the snowpeople while the items are still soft. Piles of snowballs complete the picture.

# Dressing Figures

The way in which you dress your figures will depend very much on the time you have to spend. Simple outfits can be made very easily using ring cutters, more time-consuming pleats and gathers give a fuller garment. Hats can be just the right thing to give character. Here are a few helpful ideas for hats, scarves, mittens, shoes and boots.

## Materials

Coloured modelling paste (see page 5)
Sugarpaste glue (see page 5)
Gold paste food colouring
Lustre dusting powder

## Equipment

Curved-blade modelling tool
Lace cutter
Texture sheet
Tea strainer or clay gun
Fine scissors

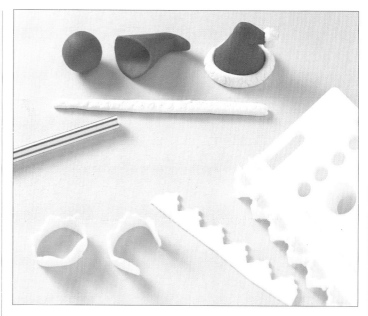

### Santa's hat

**1** Mould a ball of red paste into a long cone and hollow out the wide end until it will fit over the head. (The size of head you have to cover will determine the size of the piece of paste you use for the hat.)

**2** Roll a thin sausage of white paste long enough to fit around the bottom edge of the hat and score along it with a curved-blade tool or the end of a drinking straw. Attach with sugarpaste glue. Attach a small ball of white paste to the pointed end. Ease the hat gently over the head while it is still soft.

### Party hats and crowns

**3** Roll out a piece of white paste and cut a strip with a lace cutter. Cut sections to the size required and attach to the heads. Crowns can be painted gold or dusted with lustre powder colour.

### Woolly hats and scarves

**4** Roll a ball of paste into a cone shape and hollow out the thick end to fit over the head. Insert a finger and roll the paste gently over a texture sheet. Score around the edge. For a pompom, push some paste through a tea strainer or the fine mesh of a clay gun.

**5** Scarves are made by cutting thin strips and texturing in the same way. Cut the ends with fine scissors to look like tassels. Attach while soft.

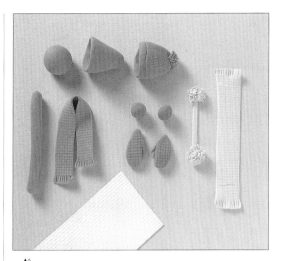

**6** Mittens are simply a small flattened cone with a piece cut out for the thumb. These can also be textured. Tiny balls or pompoms of paste with a strip of paste between them make simple earmuffs.

### Shoes and boots

**7** It is advisable to make shoes and boots from flower paste if the figure is to stand as this gives a stronger base. Mould a ball of paste to a cone of the required size. Pinch at the thick end to form the front of the shoe. Stroke the back of the paste with thumb and index finger to mould a heel. The tapered ankle shape should fit neatly inside trousers.

**8** Boots are made in a similar way but the paste is opened out at the ankle to fit on the outside of the trousers. A small fluted cone can be inserted into the boots for socks. Tiny strips of paste are used for the bootlaces.

39

# Christmas Miniatures

When using figures and models on Christmas cakes a number of little extras can be added for a more festive look. Here's how to make some of those used in this book.

## Christmas Cakes

### Materials

60g (2oz) white modelling paste (see page 5)

### Equipment

2.5cm (1 inch) round cutter
Curved-end tweezers
Red food colouring pen

**1** Roll out 60g (2oz) white modelling paste to a thickness of about 1cm (½ inch). Cut eight 2.5cm (1 inch) circles.

Pinch around the top edge of each circle with the tweezers.

**2** When dry, write 'Noel' on each cake and add dots of colour around the top with a food colouring pen.

## Christmas Puddings

### Materials

60g (2oz) two-tone brown modelling paste (see page 32)
30g (1oz) white modelling paste
Sugarpaste glue (see page 5)
Small pieces of red and green modelling paste

### Equipment

2.5cm (1 inch) blossom cutter
Broderie anglaise cutter
Craft knife or scalpel
No. 2 piping tube (tip)

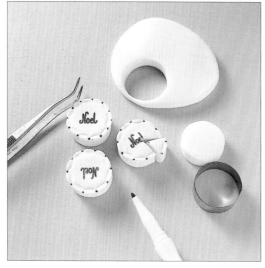

**1** ▷ Divide the brown paste into eight equal-sized pieces and roll each into a smooth ball. For the sauce, roll out some white paste and cut eight 2.5cm (1 inch) blossoms. Glue one on to the top of each pudding.

**2** ▷ The tiny holly leaves are cut with a broderie anglaise cutter from rolled-out green paste. With a craft knife or scalpel, cut two tiny V shapes out of the sides of each leaf shape and indent the centre so that they look like holly leaves.

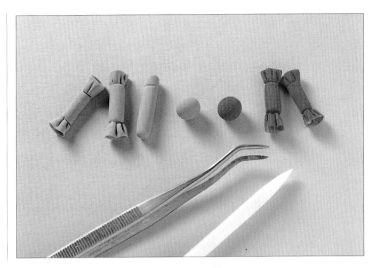

**3** ▷ The berries are cut with a no. 2 piping tube from a piece of rolled-out red paste. Attach three leaves and berries to the top of each pudding.

# Crackers

## Materials

Small pieces of red and green modelling paste (see page 5)

## Equipment

Scraper
Fine skewer or modelling pin
Tweezers

**1** ▷ Roll a small piece of modelling paste into an even sausage shape using a scraper. Score around the paste about a quarter of the way in from the ends.

**2** ▷ Open each end out with a skewer and thin. Pinch the ends gently with tweezers to create tiny folds.

# Waiting for Santa

Extend your modelling skills with these charming sleeping children.

## Materials

185g (6oz) white modelling
paste (see page 5)
Green, brown and cream paste
food colourings
Sugarpaste glue (see page 5)
Softened modelling paste (see
page 5)

## Equipment

4cm (1½ inch) round cutter
Texture sheet
Frilling tool or cocktail stick
· (toothpick)

### Bodies and legs

**1** Colour 125g (4oz)
modelling paste flesh-
coloured (see page 5) and make
an all-in-one body shape (see
page 7) using 30g (1oz) paste.

While still soft, bend the body so
that the figure is sitting, and
cross one leg over the other.

**2** Repeat to make a second
body, this time crossing
the legs the opposite way. Set
aside to dry, supporting if necessary.

### Arms

**3** Using flesh-coloured
paste, make two pairs of
arms (see page 7). Check that
the small posts at the shoulder
fit into the arm holes on the bodies. Leave to dry.

### Nightdresses

**4** Roll out a thin piece of
white paste and cut a rectangle about 10cm (4 inches)

long and 7.5cm (3 inches) wide.
Form soft pleats or gathers.
Using a rolling pin, flatten the
top half of the gathers and cut
off the surplus paste.

**5** Paint sugarpaste glue
sparingly on the back of
the flattened gathers and fold
gently around one of the figures.
Attach the arms to the body with
softened modelling paste.

**6** For the yoke, roll out and
cut a 4cm (1½ inch) circle
of white paste, and press on to
the texture sheet. Frill around
the edge by rolling with a frilling
tool or cocktail stick and drape
over the shoulders. Secure with
glue. Roll two small balls of
white paste, flatten and place at
the neck of each figure. Make a
hole through each for the neck.

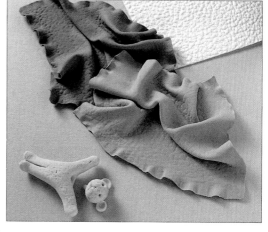

**7** Repeat steps 4–6 to dress the second figure, attaching the arms with softened modelling paste.

## Heads

**8** Following the instructions on page 20, make two heads with closed eyes. Using brown paste, cut two hair pieces and attach one to each head. When thoroughly dry, attach to the bodies with softened modelling paste.

## Blankets

**9** Colour about 15g (½ oz) modelling paste light green. Roll it out and cut out a piece about 15cm (6 inches) square. Texture and frill around the edge. While soft, arrange the blanket loosely on a board and sit one figure on top of it.

**10** Make a second, dark green blanket and drape this one around the shoulders of the other figure. Sit the second figure beside the first.

## Teddy

**11** With cream modelling paste, make a tiny teddy bear using the all-in-one body shape technique shown on page 6. Instructions for making the head are given on page 22.

## Finishing

**12** Tiny Christmas stockings and hot water bottles (see page 30) complete the scene.

# Reindeer Vacation

These relaxing reindeer, taking a well-earned rest after a busy Christmas Eve, will be very popular with children.

## Materials

250g (8oz) white modelling paste (see page 5)
Cream, brown, green and red paste food colourings
Raw dried spaghetti
Sugarpaste glue (see page 5)
Softened modelling paste (see page 5)

## Equipment

Curved-blade modelling tool
Ball modelling tool
Thin skewer or modelling pin
Texture sheet

### Reindeer head

**1** Colour 185g (6oz) modelling paste dark cream. To make the first head (Rudolph's), mould a 15g (½oz) piece of cream paste into a smooth ball. Place the ball in the palm of one hand and, with the index finger of the other hand, roll the ball shape slightly off centre so that a snout with a bulbous end forms.

**2** Further shape the head to form a short neck, and insert a piece of spaghetti. Mark the surface of the head with the curved-blade tool to give the impression of fur.

**3** To make the ears, form two small cones of cream paste and glue one to either side of the head, indenting at the base with the ball tool. Pierce four holes in the head, two on the top to hold the antlers and two lower down for the eyes. Make a fifth small hole at the end of the snout for the nose.

**4** Mould two small flattened oval shapes for the eyelids and cut some tiny eyelashes from dark brown paste. Attach the eyelids and lashes with glue. Mould and attach a small red nose. Set aside to dry.

### Body

**5** Roll a 45g (1½oz) piece of cream paste into a sausage that is thicker at one end. Roll again more firmly towards the thinner end to allow a bulb to form (this will be the feet).

**6** Pinch out the paste at either side of the thicker top to form the front legs. Roll each leg gently, allowing a rounded end to form for the front feet.

**7** Press firmly with a thin skewer or modelling pin on the centre front of the body shape to form the hind legs. To shape the hooves, press a ball tool into the ends of the legs to cup them. Score around each leg to mark the top of the hoof.

**8** Make a hole in the top of the body for the neck. Mark all over with a curved-blade tool for the hair and allow to dry thoroughly. Paint the hooves dark brown with diluted brown colouring. After drying,

they can be brushed with confectioner's glaze to give them a shine.

## Antlers

**9** Colour about 7g (¼oz) modelling paste dark brown. Mould a small piece into a shape similar to the end of a golf club. Make three indentations in the thick end, then cut away the flattened sections. Gently curve the antler and allow to dry thoroughly. Repeat to make a second antler.

## Finishing

**10** Repeat steps 1-9 to make two more reindeer with brown noses. Use softened modelling paste to assemble the reindeer and attach the antlers, arranging the heads and legs slightly differently each time (see photo below). Support with foam if necessary.

**11** The towels are made by rolling together strips of paste in alternate colours and then texturing.

45

# Templates

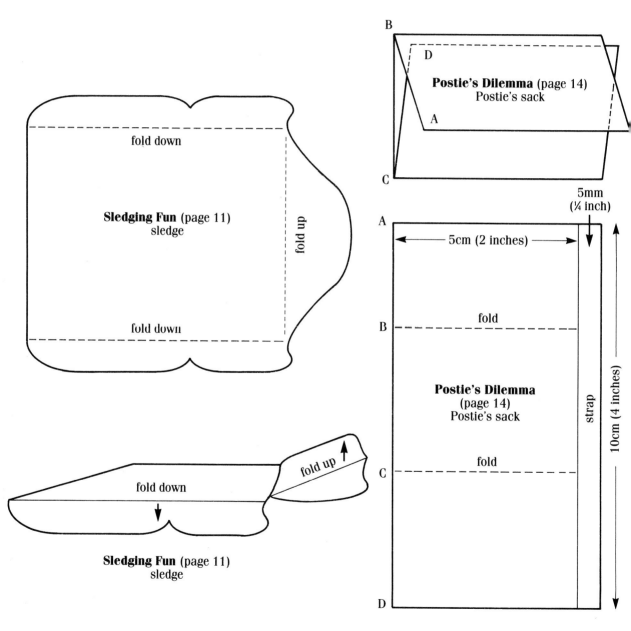

**Postie's Dilemma** (page 14)
Postie's sack

**Sledging Fun** (page 11)
sledge

fold down

fold up

fold down

fold down

fold up

**Sledging Fun** (page 11)
sledge

5mm
(¼ inch)

5cm (2 inches)

**Postie's Dilemma**
(page 14)
Postie's sack

strap

fold

fold

10cm (4 inches)

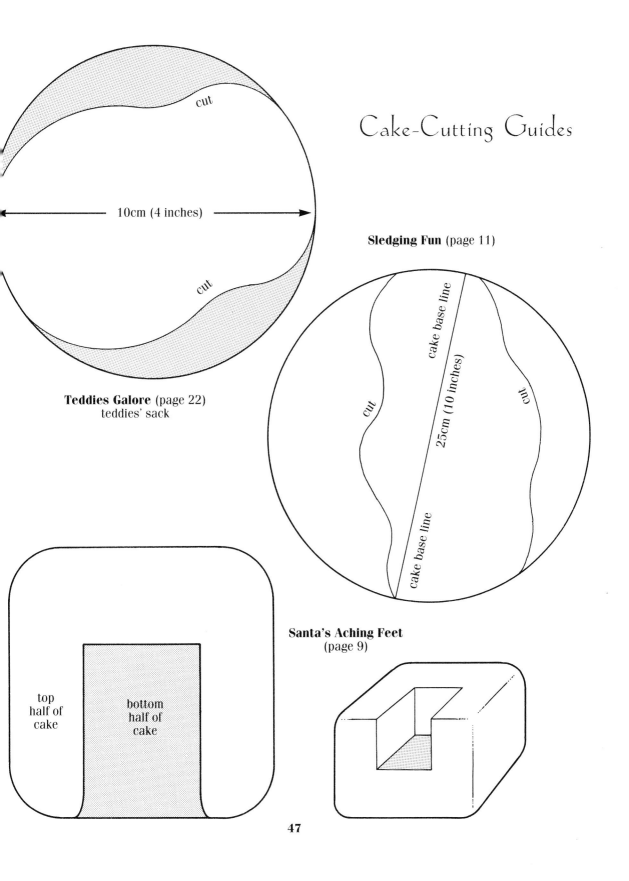

Cake-Cutting Guides

cut

cut

10cm (4 inches)

**Sledging Fun** (page 11)

**Teddies Galore** (page 22)
teddies' sack

cake base line

25cm (10 inches)

cut

cut

cake base line

cake base line

**Santa's Aching Feet**
(page 9)

top
half of
cake

bottom
half of
cake

# Acknowledgements

The author would like to thank the following for their help in the production of this book: George Hosgood and Terry Wood for their continued support and friendship; Debbie Welsh for her help and expertise.

The author and publishers would like to thank the following suppliers:

**D.I.Y. Icing Centre**
(equipment),
8 Edwards Road, Erdington,
Birmingham B24 9EP

**Renshaw Scott Ltd.**
(Regalice),
Crown Street,
Liverpool L8 7RF

**E.T. Webb,**
18 Meadow Close,
Woodley,
Stockport SK6 1QZ

**Celcakes**
(Celpins, Celtex, etc.),
Springfield House,
Gate Helmsley,
York,
North Yorkshire YO4 1NF

**Culpitt Cake Art**
(boxes, boards, etc.),
Culpitt Ltd.,
Jubilee Industrial Estate,
Ashington,
Northumberland NE63 8UQ

**Orchard Products,**
51 Hallyburton Road,
Hove,
East Sussex BN3 7GP

**Guy, Paul & Co. Ltd.**
Unit B4,
Foundry Way,
Little End Road,
Eaton Socon,
Cambs. PE19 3JH

**Squires Kitchen**
Squires House,
3 Waverley Lane,
Farnham,
Surrey GU9 8BB